GARBO

Illustrations from
International Magazine Service (IMS), Stockholm .
Pressens Bild AB, Stockholm
Europa-Press AB, Stockholm
United Press International (UPI), Stockholm

MGM film pictures are reproduced by courtesy of
"Filmhistoriska Samlingarna", Stockholm

Garbo, © 1971 by Ture Sjolander/Askild & Kärnekull, Publishers
Inc., Stockholm. All rights reserved. Art Director: Gösta Eriksson.
Printed in Sweden by Esselte Tryck 1971 for Harper & Row,
Publishers. No part of this book may be used or reproduced in
any manner whatsoever without written permission except in the
case of brief quotations embodied in critical articles and reviews. For
information address Harper & Row, Publishers, Inc., 40 East 33rd
Street, New York, N. Y. 100 16. Published simultaneously in Can-
ada by Fitzhenry & Whiteside Limited, Toronto.

FIRST EDITION
STANDARD BOOK NUMBER: 06-013926-9
LIBRARY OF CONGRESS CATALOG CARD NUMBER:
73-160651

GARBO

Ture Sjolander

HARPER & ROW, PUBLISHERS

NEW YORK · EVANSTON · LONDON

The "truth" about Garbo

The stories, observations, descriptions, analyses and interpretations of Garbo are legend alone, and contrast sharply with the lack of information from Garbo herself. Distorted by rumour, guess, error or motive the real Garbo remains silent and elusive.

And yet **is** Garbo really that difficult to see and comprehend. Perhaps all we need to do is look. The truth about Garbo is in pictures. As she looks and appears so she is. Garbo's life and times and personality are in photographs. They are her biography. In this way Garbo has contributed to this book. Other contributors, known and unknown, quoted and unquoted are also sincerely thanked.

Ture Sjolander

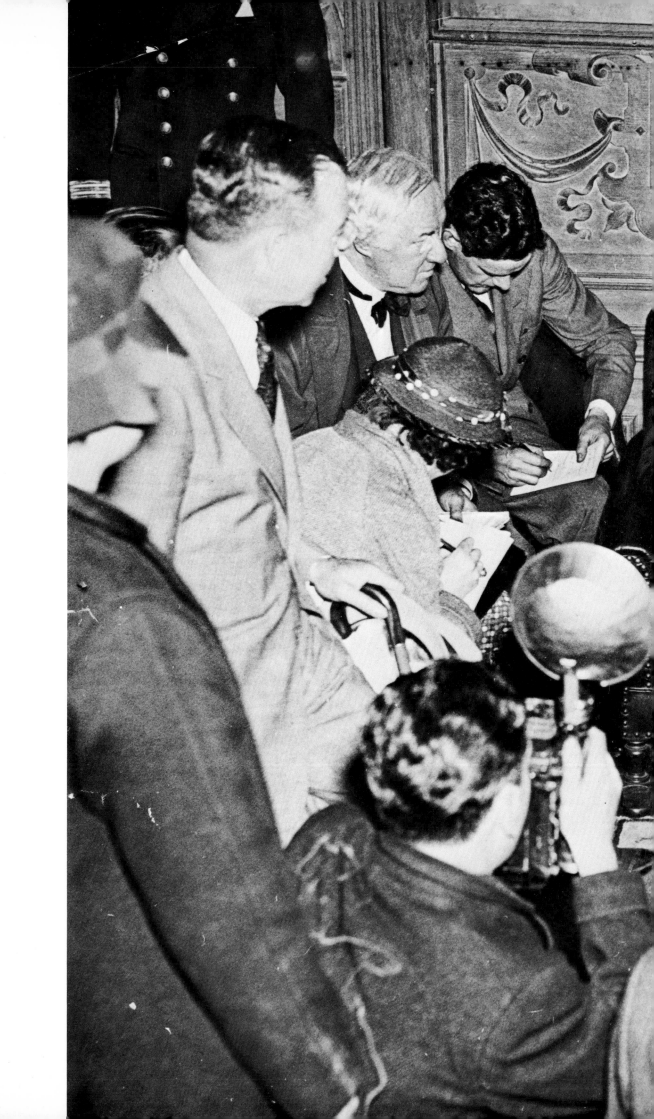

1966

1955

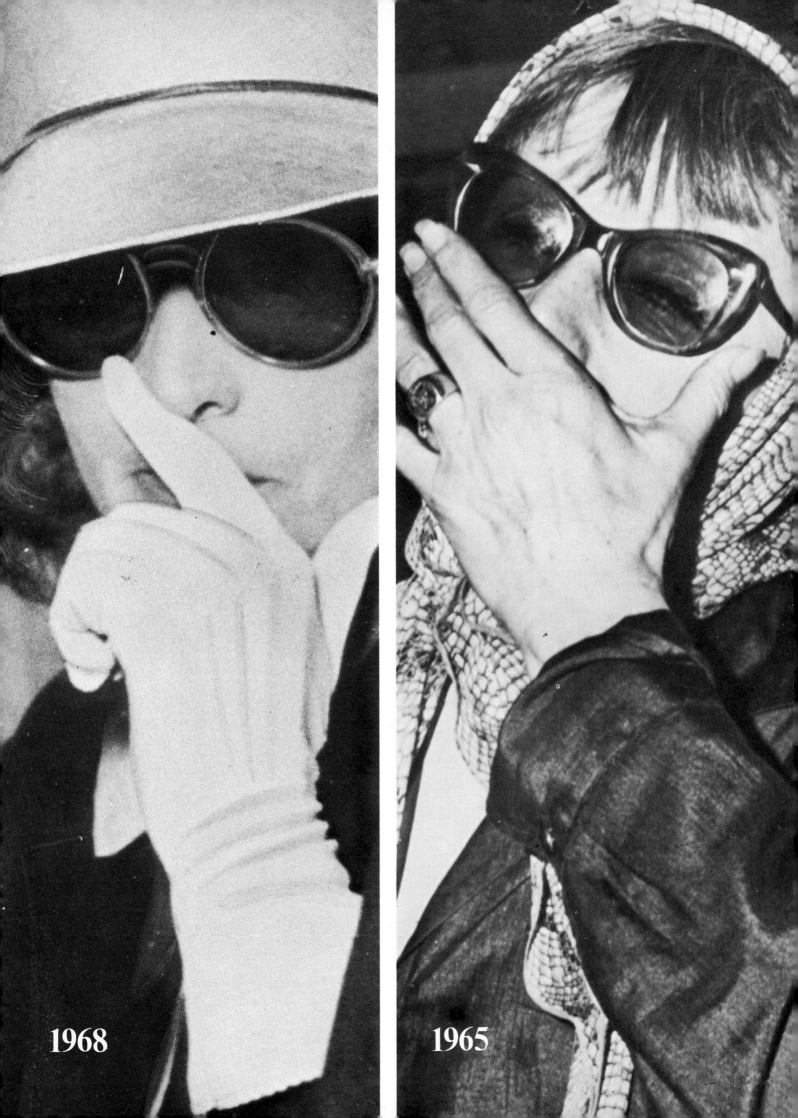

1968

1965

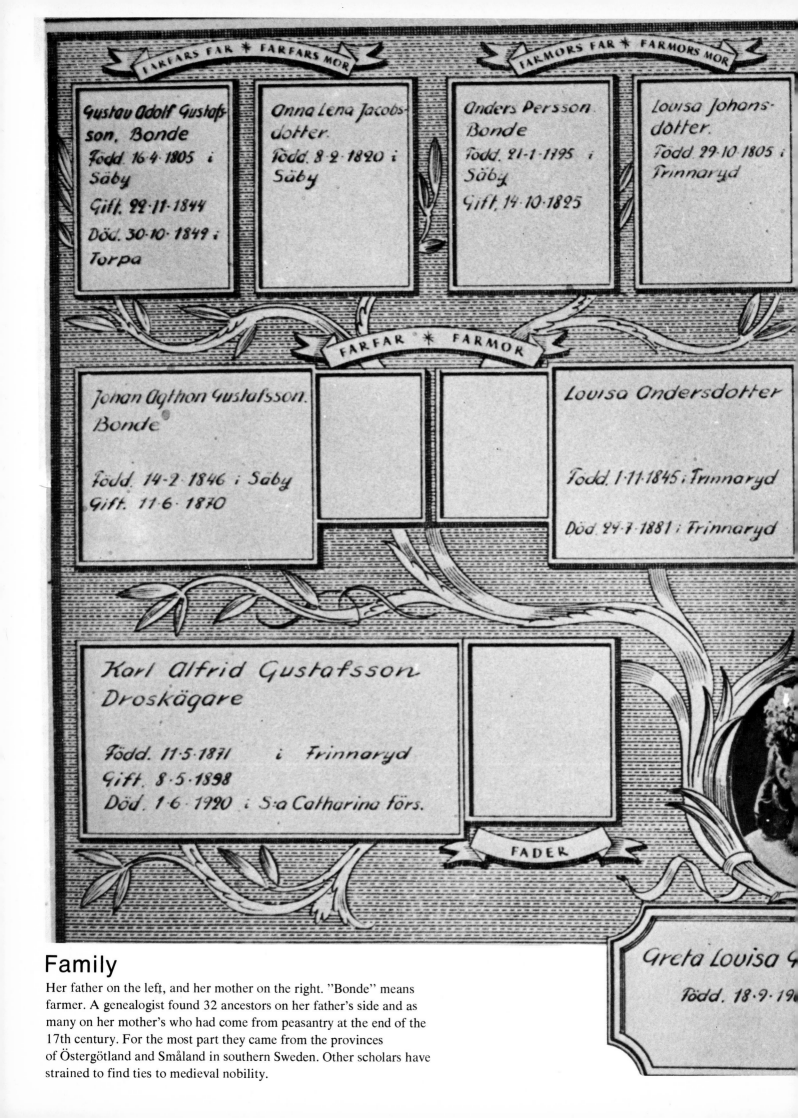

Gustav Adolf Gustafsson, Bonde
Född. 16·4·1805 i Säby
Gift. 22·11·1844
Död. 30·10·1849 i Torpa

Anna Lena Jacobsdotter.
Född. 8·2·1820 i Säby

Anders Persson Bonde
Född. 21·1·1795 i Säby
Gift. 14·10·1825

Louisa Johansdotter.
Född. 29·10·1805 i Trinnaryd

FARFAR ✲ FARMOR

Johan Agthon Gustafsson. Bonde
Född. 14·2·1846 i Säby
Gift. 11·6·1870

Louisa Andersdotter
Född. 1·11·1845 i Trinnaryd
Död. 24·7·1881 i Trinnaryd

Karl Alfrid Gustafsson. Droskägare
Född. 11·5·1871 i Frinnaryd
Gift. 8·5·1898
Död. 1·6·1920 i S:a Catharina förs.

FADER

Greta Louisa G
Född. 18·9·19

Family

Her father on the left, and her mother on the right. "Bonde" means farmer. A genealogist found 32 ancestors on her father's side and as many on her mother's who had come from peasantry at the end of the 17th century. For the most part they came from the provinces of Östergötland and Småland in southern Sweden. Other scholars have strained to find ties to medieval nobility.

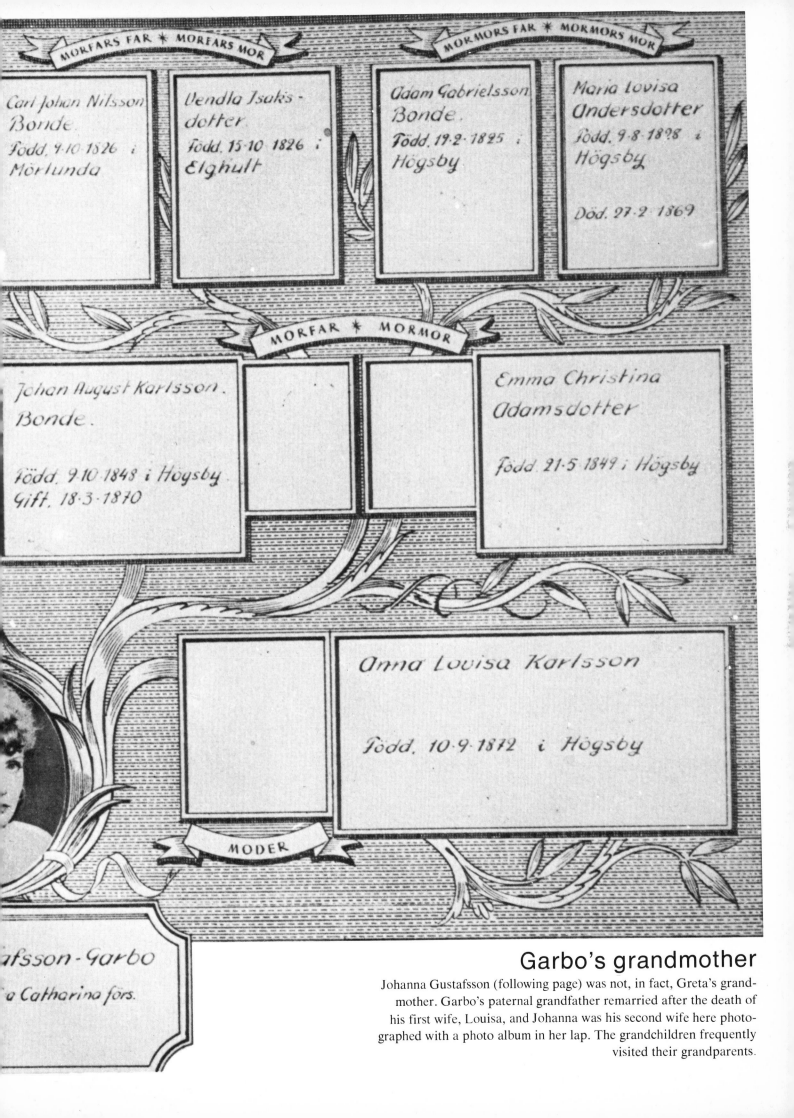

Carl Johan Nilsson
Bonde.
Född. 9·10·1826 i
Mörlunda

Vendla Isaks-
dotter.
Född. 15·10·1826 i
Elghult

Adam Gabrielsson
Bonde.
Född. 19·2·1825 i
Högsby

Maria Lovisa
Andersdotter
Född. 9·8·1828 i
Högsby

Död. 27·2·1869

MORFAR ✻ MORMOR

Johan August Karlsson.
Bonde.

Född. 9·10·1848 i Högsby
Gift. 18·3·1870

Emma Christina
Adamsdotter

Född. 21·5·1849 i Högsby

Anna Lovisa Karlsson

Född. 10·9·1872 i Högsby

MODER

...afsson-Garbo
...a Catharina förs.

Garbo's grandmother

Johanna Gustafsson (following page) was not, in fact, Greta's grand-mother. Garbo's paternal grandfather remarried after the death of his first wife, Louisa, and Johanna was his second wife here photographed with a photo album in her lap. The grandchildren frequently visited their grandparents.

Early Silence

Grandfather Johan Agathon Gustafsson with his wife Johanna (p. 17) and sons Karl and David (above). The family moved to many new places and jobs over the years. Greta's paternal uncle (above, right) bought his first taxi-cab in 1910. His friends called him Garbo-Gustaf. When Garbo was a rising star and being seen with Mauritz Stiller, the wellknown director, in the mid-twenties, Stockholm was a small town with only a few cabs.

"In those days I often drove Greta, Stiller and their friends", her uncle David has recounted. "Greta and I had a silent agreement that we wouldn't show that we knew each other on such occasions."

Mother: Anna Louisa Gustafsson
After the Second World War broke out in Europe, Garbo
brought her to California.

Father: Karl Alfred Gustafsson
Died June 1st, 1920, the year Greta celebrated her 15th
birthday.

Greta Louisa Gustafsson
was confirmed on June 13, 1920.

13/6 1920

ATELIER GÖTA
Götgatan 71
STOCKHOLM

19

Gustafsson, Greta Lovisa, född den 18 Sept. 1905 i

Målsman: Arbetaren Karl Alfred G n.

	Inskriven:		Tiden för betygens givande	Antal dagars frånvaro:						Antal dagars närvaro	Betyg för												teckning						
n:r	år och dag	församlings skola		skolkning	sjukdom	utan kläder	hinder	lov	Summa		uppförande	flit	förståndsutv.	kristendom	läsning	skrivning	räkning	geografi	historia	naturkunn.	geometri	välskrivning	frihands-	linear-	mönster-	sång	gymnastik	vapenövning huslig ekonomi	slöjd	bokföring
8571	12 22/12	Katarina s	12 22/12	1					1	104	A	A	ba									b		ba		b+				
	13 6/6		13 6	4					4	121	A	A	ba									b+		ba+		ba				
	13 20/12		13 20/12	2		3			5	100	A	A	ba									b+ b		ba b		ba				
	14 15/6		14 15/6						–	125	A	A	ba									ba b		ba b		ba				
	14 19/12		14 19/12	1					1	104	A	A	ab									ba b		ab b		ba				
	15 5/6		15 5/6						–	125	A	A	ab	ab	ab	ab	ba	ba		ab ab		ab b+		ab b		ab				
	15 20/12		15 20/12	4					4	101	A	A	ab	ab	ab	ab	ba	ab	ab	ab		ab b+		ab b		ab				
	16 14/6		16 14/6						–	125	A	A	ab	ab	ab	ab	ab	ab	ab	ab		ab b+		ab b		ab				
	16 20/12		16 20/12						–	104	A	A	ab	ab	ab	ab	ba	ab	ab	ab		ab b		ba b		ab				
	17 15/6		17 15/6	2					2	119	A	A	ab	ab	ab	ab	ba	ab	ab	ab		ab b		ba ba		ab				
	17 20/12		17 20/12	3					3	95	A	A	ab	a	ab	ab	ba	ab	ab	ab		ba b		ba ba		ab				
	18 16/6		18 16/6	1					1 2	118	A	A	ab	a	b	ab	b	ab	ab	ab		ab b		ba ba+ ab						
	18 20/12		18 20/12				7		7	80	A	A	ab	a	ab	ab	ba	ab	ab	ab		ab b		ab ba baab B						
	19 14/6		19 14/6						–	117	A	A	Ab	a	a	a	Ba	a	a	a		a B		ab ba ab ab Ba						

School days

In Katarina Södra primary school 1919, (previous double-page spread), fourteen-year-old Greta is the third from the right in the second row from the front.

All of Garbo's grades in school (1912—1919) have been preserved in the school's records. The highest grade was an A, then came a, AB and Ba. B meant passing. Greta received no failing grades. In her last term, she got an A in Christianity and a in reading, writing, geography, history and science. In arithmetic she got a Ba. The grades in the first three columns are for "behavior", "diligence" and "maturity". In the first two an A was normal for a well-behaved pupil. The seven subjects on the right include penmanship, art, singing, athletics, home economics, needlework and book-keeping.

During the spring of 1918 Greta was absent from school one day without the permission of her teacher or parents. During seven school years she missed a total of eleven days because of illness.

Alva, Greta's older sister, dressed to be confirmed. It was easy to spoil little Alva. She was so beautiful and lovable that she immediately won the affection of everybody, her uncle David has said. Alva had made a modest start on a screen career in Sweden when she died in 1926 at the age of 22. The news reached Greta in the midst of the first takes of **The Temptress.**

Sven, Greta's older brother, dressed in his suit for confirmation. Sven moved to the United States with his family during World War II. Occasionally he helped Greta with her business in Sweden and later he worked at MGM. "Her brother had a certain artistic leaning", according to one of Garbo's biographers. The same source claims that Garbo paid for his studies.

Garbo's childhood home

was at Blekingegatan 32 in the southern part of the city
of Stockholm. Garbo experts argue whether it was an
apartment of one, two or more rooms. The evidence has
been removed by bulldozers.
Garbology started in the Thirties through the first attempts
to penetrate Blekingegatan 32. Neighbors were systemati-
cally interviewed; playmates and schoolmates searched for
through newspaper ads. Her teachers have reread her
records and recalled the charm and difficulties of the
famous pupil.

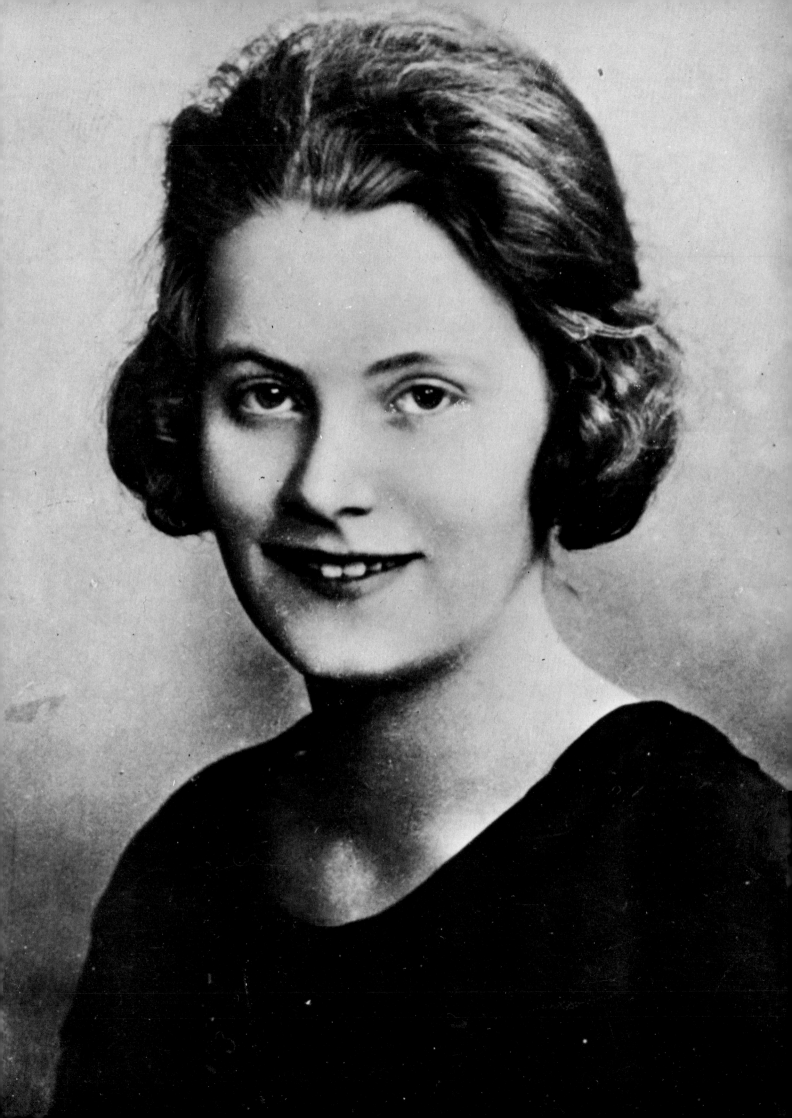

The girl in the barber shop

Many Stockholm barber shops claim Garbo worked for them during her last year of school and the following year.

The girl in the hat department

In 1920 Miss Greta Gustafsson, aged fourteen, applied for a job at PUB, one of
Stockholm's largest department stores. She was hired as a shop assistant, paying
$ 25 a month. Through her job in the hat department, she was asked one day to show
the spring models. In PUB's mail order catalog (edition: 50 000 copies) for the
spring of 1921 she wore these hats.

In 1921 she took part in a screen commercial about the department store. The
following year she ate cake in a screen commercial financed by the Consumers'
Cooperative Association of Stockholm (above, right).

In 1922 she got her first part in a feature movie. It was **Peter, the Tramp,** a comedy,
in which Miss Gustafsson played the part of one of the mayor's three daughters
(below, right). Garbo is in the middle.

Till öfverståthållareämbetet.

Garbonfinnervigfort.

Undertecknad får härmed vördsamt anhålla om tillstånd
för min omyndiga dotter fröken Greta Gustafsson att få
antaga släktnamnet Garbo.
Prästbevis bifogas.
Stockholm den 9 november 1923.
Anna Gustafsson.

Bevittnas:

Monica Mårtensson   Ragnar Eld

Min moders förestående ansökan bevittnas av mig.
Stockholm den 9 november 1923.
Greta Gustafsson.
Bevittnas:

Monica Mårtensson   Ragnar Eld

Darbo — Gábor — Garbo

"The undersigned requests hereby respectfully permission for my underage daughter, Miss Greta Gustafsson, to adopt the family name of **Garbo.***
Birth certificate enclosed.*
Stockholm, November 9, 1923
Anna Gustafsson
Witnesses
My mother's application at hand is subscribed to by me

The name Gustafsson fills pages and pages in Swedish telephone directories. After the shooting of **Peter, the Tramp** during the summer of 1922, Greta applied to the drama school of the Royal Dramatic Theater in Stockholm. She was admitted in the fall. Mona Mårtensson (right) was one of Garbo's friends from drama school. They both auditioned for Stiller. They corresponded with each other during Garbo's early period in Hollywood. Two years after Greta left for Hollywood Mona also went into the movies. Another friend from drama school and with whom Garbo corresponded was Vera Schmiterlöw who is pictured with Garbo in the film car (see next spread). After more than a year at drama school and her first part for the famous director Mauritz Stiller, the question of changing her name arose. The name "Garbo", many have said, was inspired by Erica Darbo, a Norwegian operetta performer who was much appluaded in Stockholm at the time. The Hungarian royalty name of Gàbor has also been mentioned. Many have been credited with thinking up the name, such as Stiller, his scriptwriter, the vicar who confirmed Greta and Mimi Pollak, her friend from drama school. In any case, Miss Gustafsson was the one who took the name.

Arrived!

Mauritz Stiller, the famous Swedish director, arrived in New York with his protegé Garbo in the midst of a heat wave in July, 1925. The reception committee on the pier consisted of only one free lance photographer who had been paid in advance by MGM to take a few publicity shots. They waited in New York for three months on rather limited funds before they got word from Hollywood to take a train to California.

Mauritz Stiller was reputed to be a genius and a dominating director. Destitute, he had left his native country of Finland, then a Russian grand duchy, at the age of 21 for Stockholm, where he started to work in the theater. He was already considered the most exciting film director in the country when, in 1923, he tested the almost entirely untried Garbo for the female lead in **Gösta Berling's Saga,** which was based on a novel by Swedish Nobel Prize winner Selma Lagerlöf. Stiller asked the drama school pupil to diet, yet he thought she had potentials. Greta Gustafsson, 17 years old, was signed for the female lead in the nearly four-hour movie for a total of $ 600. The reception was quite good. With Garbo and a film troupe, Stiller travelled to Turkey at the end of 1924 to make a film that was never released. On the way back some members of the troupe stopped off in Berlin where Garbo got a part in the German director G. W. Pabst's **The Street of Sorrow.**

In spring 1925, Louis B. Mayer of Metro-Goldwyn-Mayer, came to Europe. He contracted for Stiller and Garbo to come to Hollywood. In Los Angeles MGM arranged a grand reception (following two pages).

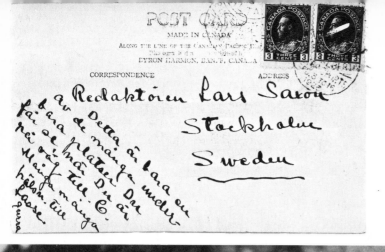

Redaktören Lars Saxon
Stockholm
Sweden

Greetings from Gurra

Garbo wrote to friends in Sweden and conveyed impressions from her first years in the new continent. On the Canadian post card she wrote
This is just one of the many wonderful places you'll see on your way to C.

> *Many many greetings to Lasse,*
> *Gurra*

Garbo seldom signed her letters "Greta". "Gurra" was a common signature; she also used "Poor Tage". Stiller with Garbo on his right among friends in Los Angeles during the first stay in Hollywood. Several friends from Stockholm were already in Hollywood. On the following two pages Garbo and Stiller have been snapped with actress Karin Molander and actor Lars Hansson with whom Greta had co-starred in **Gösta Berling's Saga.**

Waiting

to start on a film Greta met her Swedish friends who formed a sort of colony in Santa Monica. The quartet from the preceeding two pages are seen together above. Garbo's two girl friends on the following spread are Karin Molander (with sunshade) and Edith Erastoff, married to Swedish director Victor Sjöström (Seastrom), who had accepted a Hollywood offer before Stiller.

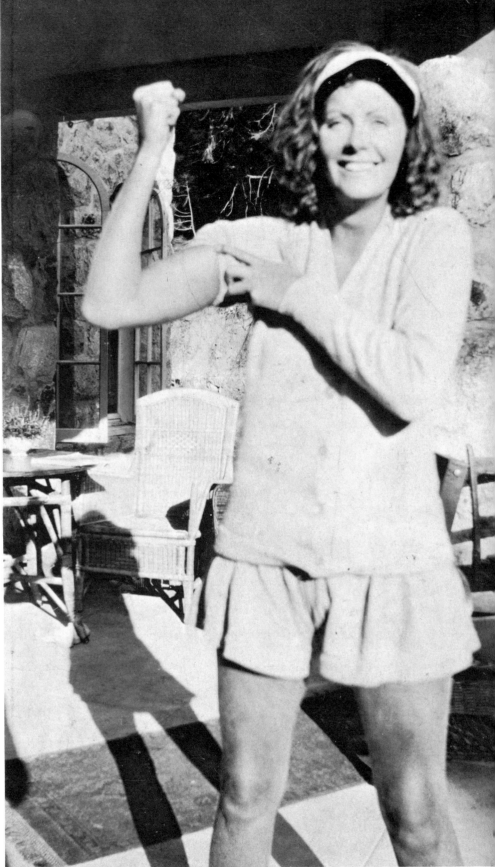

"This is a rather unusual portrait of Garbo who imagines
she has become strong by paddling about in my canoe
for a couple of hours. But she has got a sun tan." Notes
on the back of a private snapshot.

Launching

MGM was unsure at first how to launch Garbo. The girl with the lion and the smart, sporty girl on the following pages illustrate some of the attempts that were tried.
After ten weeks Garbo got her first role, largely as a result of Stiller's persuasive powers. But Stiller did not get the assignment. Garbo got the female lead in **The Torrent** and co-starred with Ricardo Cortez; Monta Bell directed. Although the movie got a chilly reception from critics, it was a success for Garbo. After a good deal of hard work for Garbo with a new language, a new director and new routines in the studio, the film was ready to open by Christmas, 1925.

A new lead, rather like the first, was quickly decided for Garbo. This time Stiller was to direct. But he had difficulty making himself understood in the studios and getting along with his superiors at MGM. Stiller was replaced by Fred Niblo who finished **The Temptress.**

It was not an optimistic young star's voice that spoke in the letters home when the film was being shot:
"I've become afraid of life . . ."
". . . It's as if someone had cut off part of me. I've tried to get permission to go home but everyone advises me not to."

MPGP-9838

Garbo's Car

will always remain Garbo's, no matter how many owners it has had. This is also the case of her house, her country estate and other things she has owned. In 1950 "Garbo's car", a 60 horsepower Dusenberg m/34, was on sale in Paris. In 1956 Garbo's Mercedes convertible 290 m/35 was on sale in Stockholm.

Garbo and the prince

"You know that the crown prince and princess Louise were here. In the Metro studios for lunch Crown Prince Gustaf Adolf had Garbo as his partner. Oh, oh, oh. I arrived 15 minutes late for lunch. Wasn't my fault that I worked — a scandal! He was very friendly and I poured out all sorts of foolish things."

In the summer of 1926, the Crown Prince and Princess of Sweden visited Hollywood on their tour of the United States. The man on the right is Mr. Robinson, president of the First National Bank of Los Angeles.

Handwriting

Graphologist Harry Teltscher commented on Garbo's handwriting in 1937 in **Neues Wienerjournal:** "What one notices, above all, in Greta Garbo's handwriting is the marked regularity. She writes her name with simple and emphatic letters. There is an obvious parallell between the regularity of her handwriting and her facial traits. The strong tie between the different letters show that Garbo thinks logically, is clear in her deliberations and calm about her decisions. Her simple manner of writing corresponds to her simple way of life, e. g. the manner in which she dresses in her private life. Her style is natural. It also reveals a powerful system of nerves, lots of energy and endurance and, to be a woman, very strong will-power. She abstains from cheap effects and can be hard as nails when it comes to true and inner values."

"...But I suppose the day will come. Well, when you sell yourself for dollars this is what happens to you. If they would only come sooner, the bastards". From a letter to book publisher Lars Saxon with whom Garbo corresponded.

kommer

dag! Ja, ja, man

t dig fri-

få för man

om den

e komma

dom djäklarna.

63

Home to Mother

At Christmas 1928, Garbo made
her first visit to Sweden since she
had come to Hollywood. She
had made seven movies in rapid
succession för MGM. Her
mother (right) and friends from
drama school days received her
in Södertälje, a city south of
Stockholm, where, naturally, the
press also boarded the train. A
big party was arranged in the
diner as Stockholm drew nearer
(next two pages). Her mother
and Garbo are in the foreground
along with Nils Lundell, the hus-
band of Mimi Pollak, Garbo's
close friend from drama school
and later one of Sweden's best
known directors.

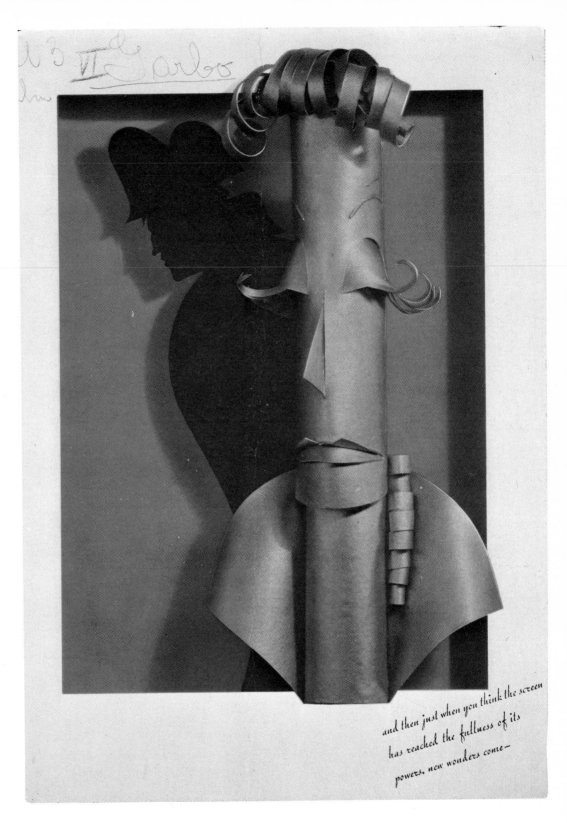

and then just when you think the screen has reached the fullness of its powers, new wonders come—

The Sphinx

"Describe Garbo", was one of many similar contests that originated from the MGM offices. "The Sphinx of the 20th century" was the winning entry: it reflected publicity slogans of Garbo's early Hollywood days. Other suggestions included "The transparent Viking girl who enchants and poisons" and "The Crystal Flower". Many entries were simply entitled "The Divine".

The face above appeared in ads for **Conquest,** the 1937 movie in which Garbo played the part of Marie Walewska and Charles Boyer played Napoleon.

Homage

On p. 72 there is a German post card, a mosaic, a Hollywood promotion drawing for Ninotschka; they all date from the 1930's. The sketch Ninotschka from 1929 dates from when she modelled for a group of artists in Stockholm. The portrait on this page is by Einar Nerman, her friend.

69/200

Einar Nerman

Caricature

A caricature from **Vanity Fair** by Cavar-rubias is on the far left. This artist's famous caricature of Garbo and Calvin Coolidge was bought at an auction by Garbo's long-time companion George Schlee. It has been assumed that he bought it on Garbo's behalf.

Next to it is an Italian caricature, exhibited at the Film Olympics in Venice in 1935. The woman on the left (right-hand page) is made of wax.

The idol

Wood carvings of Garbo's head were mass produced in
Germany in 1933. Exhibitions, festivals and contests on
the theme of Garbo were common during the Thirties.
Here are the finalists in a contest "Hungary's Greta
Garbo" in 1931. The winner is on the far right.

"Leave me alone"

"There is no star who knows so instinctively when she is good in a photo", said Clarence Bull, who in 1934 celebrated the fact he had taken all 3,000 publicity shots of Garbo for MGM. Outside the studios Garbo has always fled as far as possible from photographers. In this picture, taken in New York in 1938, she is seen with Robert Rued.

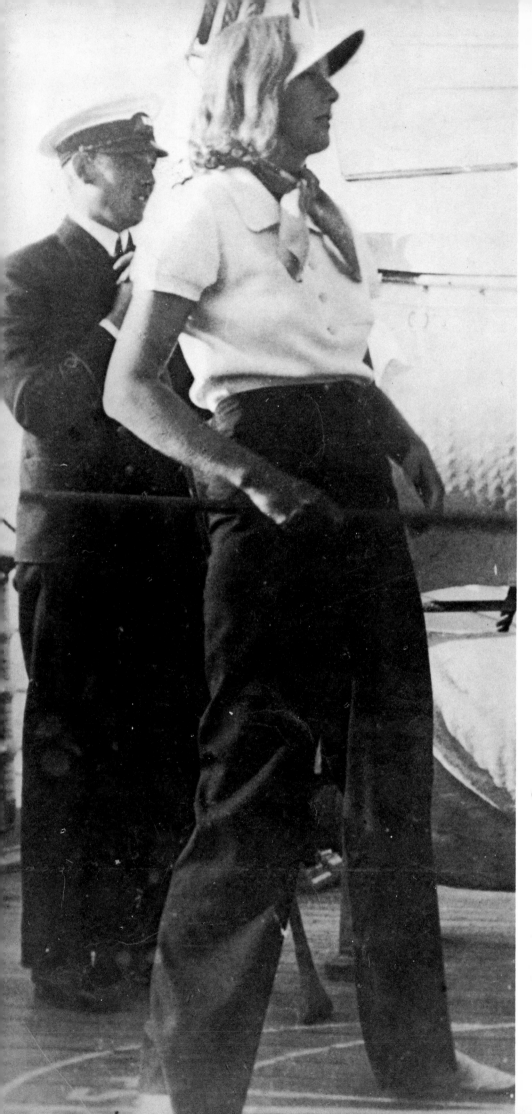

On board

Atlantic passenger liners were favorite hunting grounds for journalists. They have followed "Greta Bakke", "J. Emerson", "Phyllis Smith", "Beatrice Wills", "Helene Morgan", "Miss Hansen", "Carin Lundh", "J. Clark", "Harriet Brown" and the other pseudonyms Garbo used in the vain hope of getting the big scoop — an exclusive interview. Amateur photographers have often been more successful. Here is Garbo on her way to Sweden in 1934 (this page) and her return to New York (right).

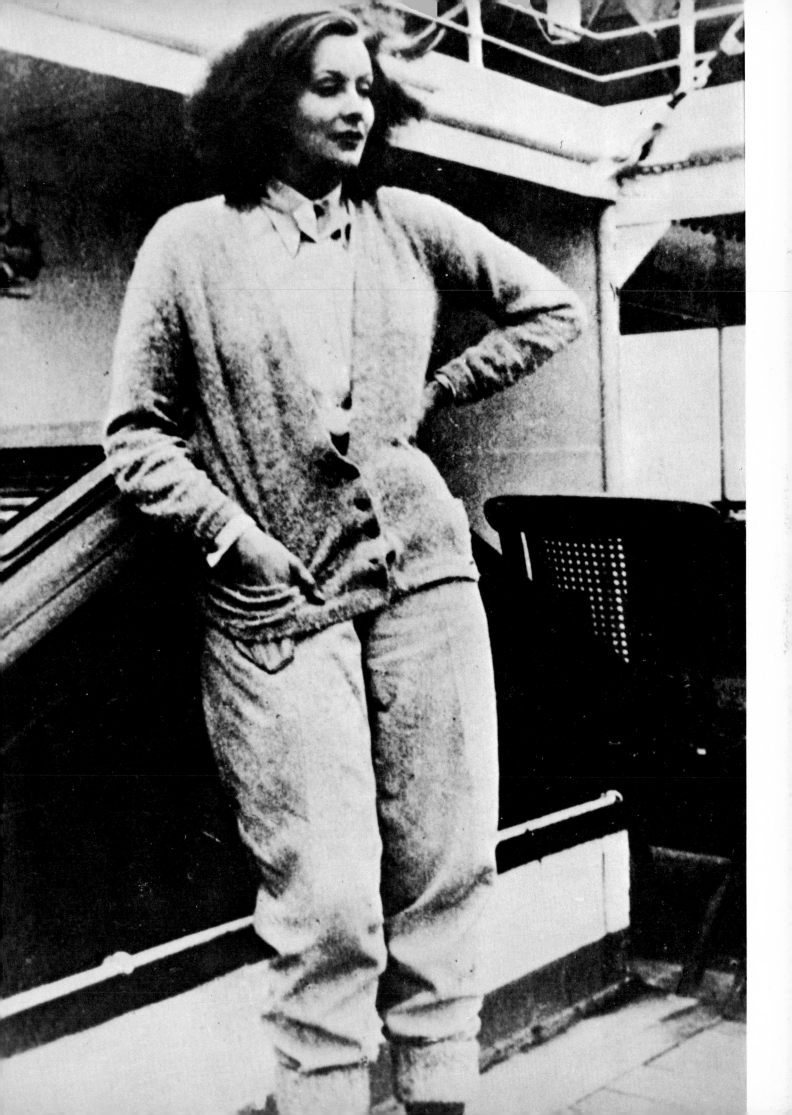

In Sweden

Garbo has been less shy of the press in her own country. Here in 1935, she is seen on board the Kungsholm approaching Gothemburg, on her third visit to Sweden.

Garbo gives short answers to all questions. Mostly she says "nothing" or "no", according to the newspaper reports of her arrival. But she definitely makes an intelligent impression, a reporter adds.

Greta Garbo is still in Sweden as newspapermen and photographers search for her in vain on board ships to The States. On April 4th, 1936 she is discovered taking a walk with friends (next double-page spread) — Count and Countess Nils Wachtmeister and the poet Fredrik Nycander.

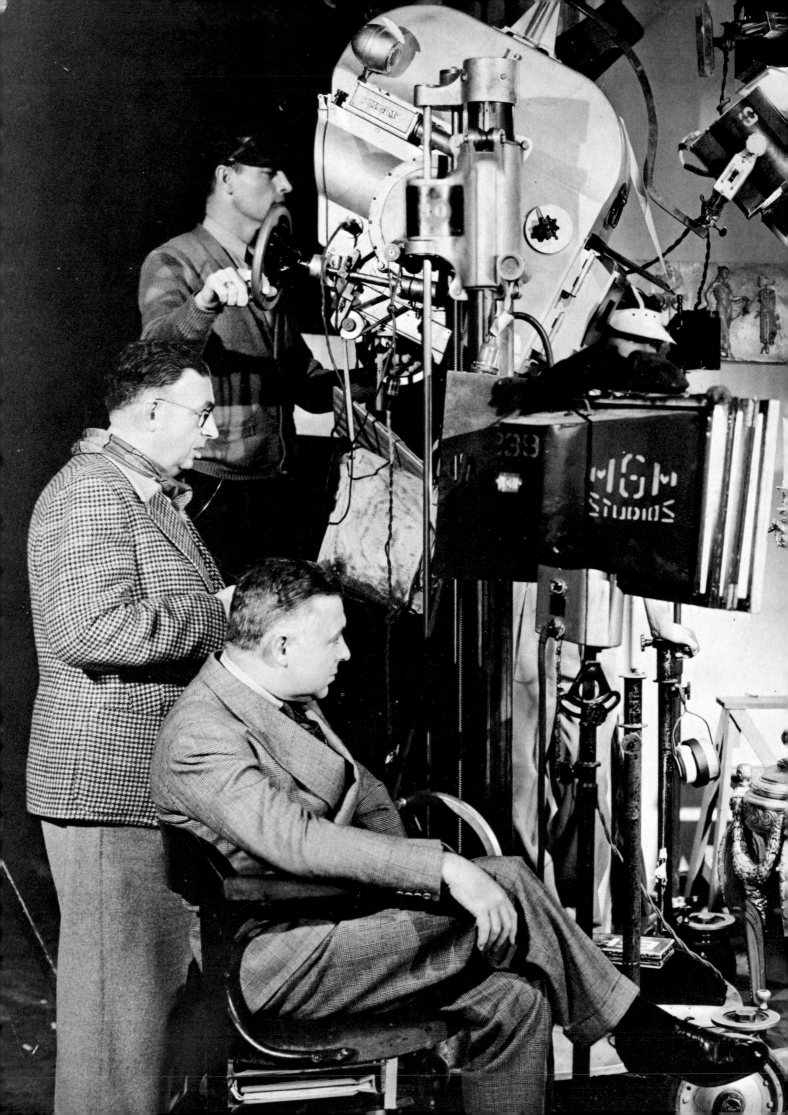

983x17
MGM

Conquest

Garbo as Marie Walewska and
Charles Boyer as Napoleon
while shooting **Conquest** in 1937.
Cameraman Karl Feund stand-
ing at left and Clarence Brown,
who directed seven of Garbo's
films, sitting immediately in
front of him.

Fashion

What Garbo is wearing was reported in complete detail on every occasion. At the congress of American hairdressers in Philadelphia, 1938, loud protests were launched against Garbo for being interviewed and photographed with long, straight hair at a time when the current fashion prescribed combing it on the crown. Later the manufacturers of silk stockings protested to her wearing woolen stockings. Shortly afterwards the ladies' tailors and the cosmetic industry expressed their displeasure. Sometime later attention was focused on "the new Garbo" once again.

Con garbo

The meaning of the Italian word "garbo" is "grace" or "politeness". The meaning cannot have been unknown to the famous conductor Leopold Stokowski. He is seen in the picture on the left with Garbo in Italy, 1937. Stokowski is one of the many men who have been presented in regular reports of her "impending marriage". In 1938 it was said they were going to make a film about Tschaikovsky together.

Garbo's diet

became another topic of discussion when Garbo was seen often with Gaylord Hauser, the dietician. When they were photographed together in Palm Beach in 1940 (next double-page spread) it was said that everything was set for the wedding.

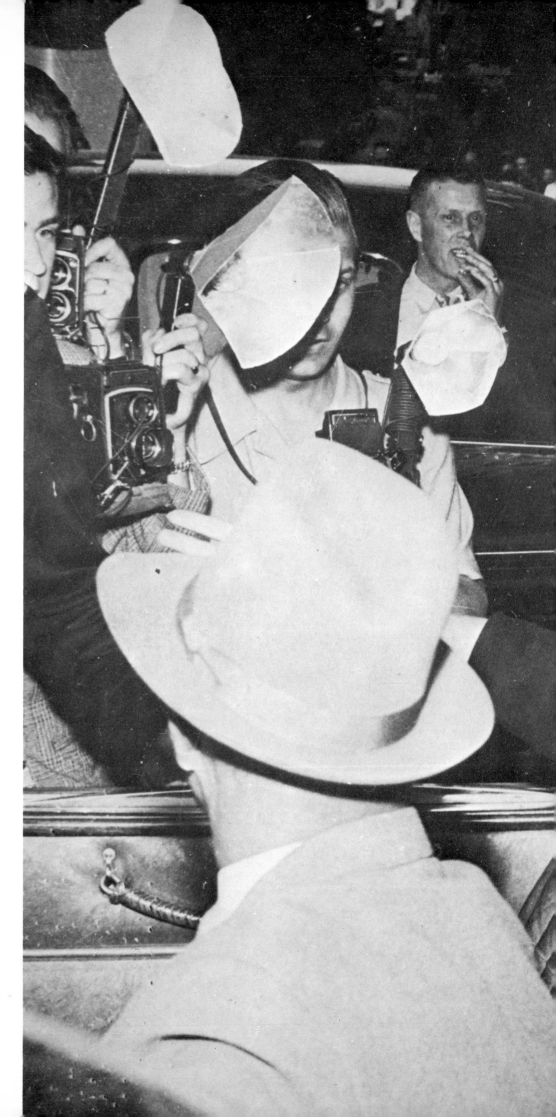

Garbo talks

was the big attraction of her first
talkie in 1930.
"Well, gentleman. As usual I
have nothing to say!" The press
conveyed this message in
headlines from her royal
reception in Stockholm, 1946.

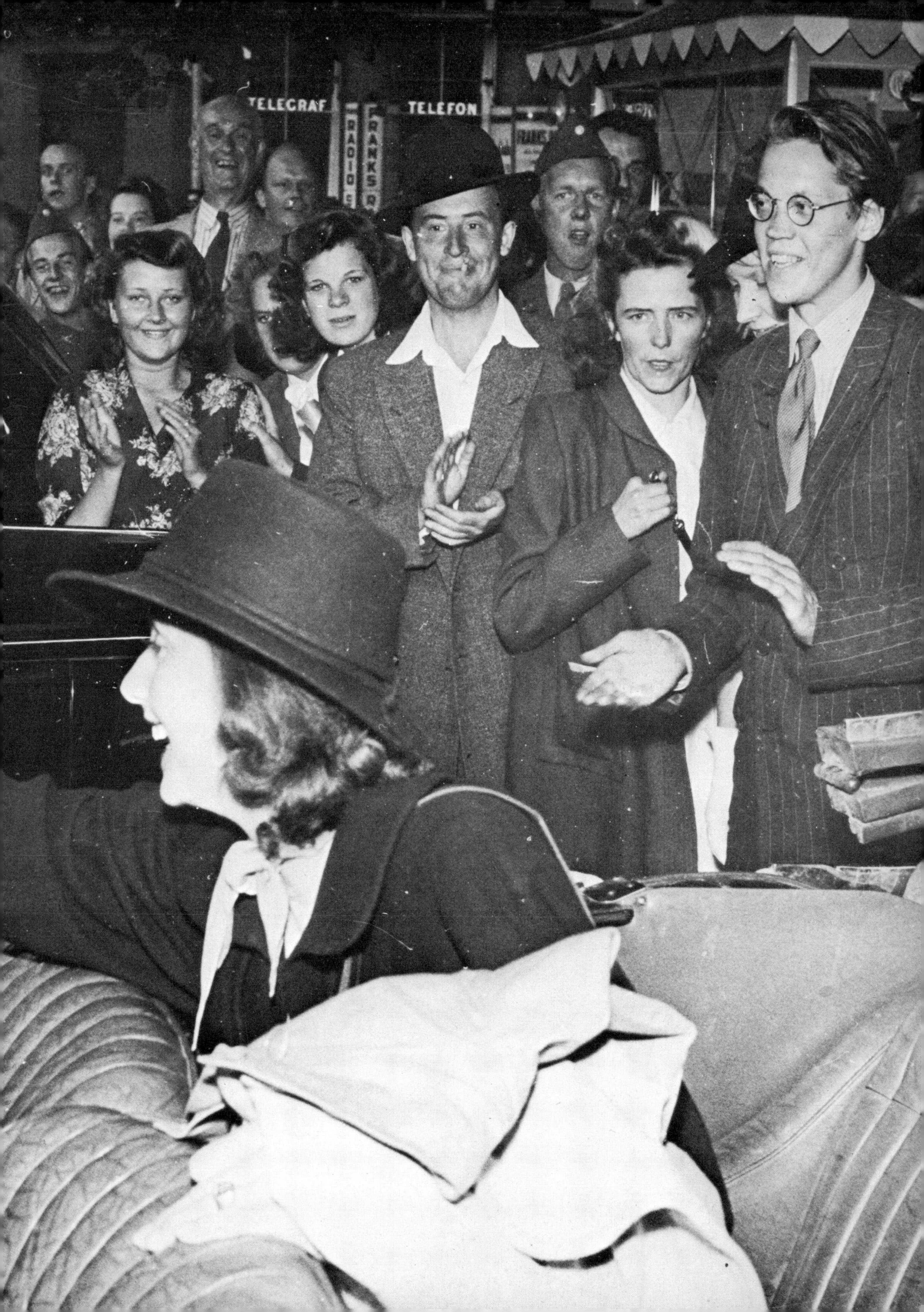
TELEGRAF
TELEFON
RADIO

Just friends

Greta Garbo crossing a Stockholm street with George Schlee. He was seen with Garbo for twenty years. They met through Schlee's wife, Valentina, Garbo's dress designer in New York. On the Riviera, in Cap d'Ail, George Schlee bought "le Roc", a spacious and well protected house, which, naturally, has never been called anything besides "Garbo's house". In 1964 George Schlee died. The house and its furniture went to Valentina, but Garbo has spent some time there since then.

Four angles of Garbo

During their visit to Stockholm in 1946, Garbo and Schlee lived with Max Gumpel. As they wanted to live incog-nito they stayed at his home in the Stockholm archi-pelago. The newspaper captions read as follows: "Every now and then Greta Garbo drives into town to go to restaurant and to the theater. Greta Garbo had dinner at Bellmansro restaurant and was in excellent spirits."

"Garbo has no special angle from which she should be photographed nor special facial expressions that she feels suit her", said Clarence Bull in 1934, after he had taken all MGM's publicity stills of her. "There isn't a star who is as anxious to see prints of the photos snapped", Bull continued.

GUEST GRETA GARBO POUTS BETWEEN BITES OF FOOD BUT HOLDS ATTENTION OF BRAZIL

USTRIALIST NELSON SEABRA AND MRS. WILLIAM RANDOLPH HEARST

Garbo on camera

"Garbo returns to the screen", "Garbo to make new movie" are headlines that have occurred frequently since she left MGM after completing **Two-Faced Woman** in 1941.

Shortly before it opened it was said that she was going to appear in a film of Tolstoys's **The Kreutzer Sonat.**

In March, 1943, she was to play the part of Saint Joan in England, and a year later she was to appear in a film about the Norwegian fleet in the war. In 1945 she was supposed to co-star with Bing Crosby in a musical, and a year later to appear in an Alexander Korda production in England, a movie about 18th century Swedish monarch Gustaf III and Sarah Bernhardt.

In 1947 she was supposed to portray George Sand, and to have rejected the lead in **The Paradine Case** at the last moment. In the spring 1949 an Italian film was "set" as well as **The Duchess of Langelais,** which Walter Wagner was going to produce. The latter was postponed over and over again, but by October it had been officially titled **Lovers and Friends.** There were many more rumours about movies than mentioned here. And they have not died out after these pictures were taken in 1949.

The Stars predict

Great fame through her own powers is what the horoscope, which astrologist C. H. Huter in Dresden, Germany, prepared in 1931 foresaw for the then 26-year-old Greta Garbo. The astrologist pointed out that she was born under the same sign as Richard Wagner (Virgo), and claimed that "the spiritually erotic rules over the sensually erotic in her life". Big success was predicted for her in 1932 and 1933.

Mittelalterlicher Holzschnitt.

Horoskop

für *Greta Garbo* *biographie*

geb. am *18. September 1905* *7* Uhr *30* Min. nach ~~mittag~~ (Wochentag *Montag*)

in *Stockholm* .... *59° 20'* nördl. Breite, *18° 5'* östl. Länge = *1 H. 12 M. 20 S.*

	H. M. S
Sternzeit in Greenwich: . . .	11. 46. 56
Korrektur für östl. Länge: .	− 12
Sternzeit des Geburtsortes:	11. 46. 44
astronom. Tag: 18.9. Geburtszeit: . .	7. 30. 0
Zonenzeit-Unterschied: . . .	+ 12. 20
Wahre Orts-Geburtszeit: . .	7. 42. 20
Umrechnung in Sternzeit: +	1. 16
Sternzeit des Geburtsortes: +	11. 46. 44
Kulminierender Punkt: . . .	19. 30. 20

Beim Mondort ist die Parallaxe mit + 0° 12' berücksichtigt worden.

Aspectarium

Pla-net	☉	☽	♆	♅	♄	♃	♂	♀	☿
☉									
☽									
♆									
♅									
♄									
♃									
♂									
♀									
☿									

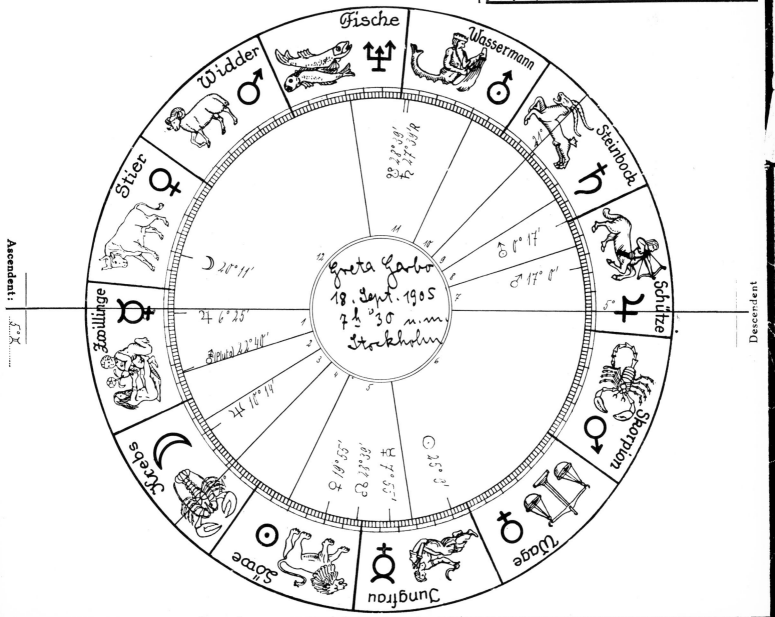

Ascendent: _5° ♍_

Descendent

Greta Garbo 18. Sept. 1905 7 h 30 n. m. Stockholm

Dark glasses

While Garbo did everything possible to avoid the press wherever she resided and travelled between New York, London, Paris, Sweden, the French Riviera and other places, journalists, authors, psychoanalists, graphologists and astrologists have strained to find new approaches. The headlines seem closely related: "The Real Garbo", "A New Slant on Garbo", "The World's Love Ideal",

"Greta Garbo's Soul", "The Saga of Greta Garbo", "My Life with Greta Garbo", "Garbo — the Life of a Star", "Garbo — the Lonely Star", "The True Story of Garbo", etc. This wealth of writing has two things in common. All the articles in some way claim to be the first to reveal some new truth about Garbo. They have also been written without any assistance from Garbo.

Suddenly

Our photographer ran into Garbo on Fifth Avenue. The
picture on the left dates from spring 1955, Garbo is accom-
panied by Philippe de Rothschild.

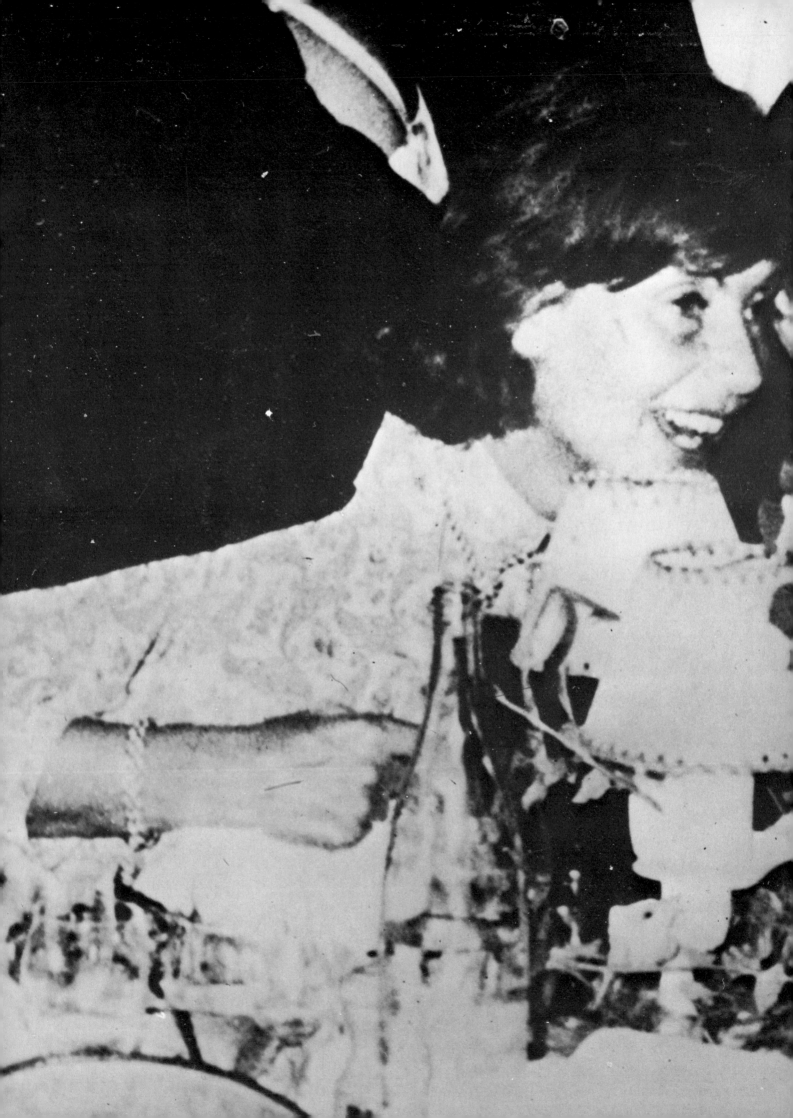

High Society

In July 1955, Garbo boarded Aristotle
Onassis' yacht, "Christina", in Monte
Carlo. Two days later they spent a day
sight-seeing on Capri. Two weeks later
they turned up in Palermo. By September
the newspapers were ready to tell how
Onassis, Garbo and Ali Khan were going
to rent a house together in Vienna to
attend the grand opening of the opera. At
the same time, it was reported that the
Christina had docked at the Greek island
of Ithaca. This photo was taken in 1956.
In July 1957, Garbo was received on her
arrival at the railway station in Nice by
a Hungarian orchestra in red coats, which
Onassis had arranged. In 1958, Winston
Churchill went aboard the yacht for a
lunch with Onassis and Garbo.

Garbo laughs

"Garbo's sweater and the scarf around her neck contrasted
shockingly with the pearl-adorned decolletes at the Sporting
Club", a newspaper reported from Monaco in 1958.

Walks

"Guess who I saw on the street today!" All attempts to map out how Garbo spends her days result in accounts of a daily routine with regular and long walks. Garbo on the street, Garbo at a shop window, Garbo going through a door and similar acts account for most Garbo snapshots. During her Hollywood days it was jokingly said that the only person who had seen the inside of her house was a housebreaker. On that occasion Garbo escaped by way of the drain pipes.

Big game

On this occasion in Paris, 1959, things were relatively
calm. The well-known Garbo hunt has often taken rather
dramatic forms, and the tricks used to avoid the
photographers sometimes seem inspired by Hollywood.
It is a story of long sieges, frustrated coups, and escapes
through backdoors. In the escape from the photograpers
in Rome, 1949, Garbo's car, which was driven by a former
French pilot, was stopped several times for traffic
misdemeanors. But the police forgot the fines when they
recognized Garbo.

Passport

After a visit with Prime Minister Anthony Eden at 10 Downing Street, Garbo is seen walking with photographer Cecil Beaton in October, 1956.

"We were friends in those days. I never asked to take her picture as I knew that was the last thing she wanted", Cecil Beaton has said. But one day Garbo said: "If you just hadn't been such a big and famous photographer..."

"Then you would let me take a passport picture of you", Beaton filled in.

Beaton apparently knew that Garbo's passport was about to expire. He was allowed to take the photos of which two are printed on the following pages. Later, when Beaton let the photos be published, he was very critical of Garbo. He said, among other things, that she was unable to experience friendship and unable to sacrifice anything for another person.

Miss G

Garbo's apartment overlooks the East River from the fifth floor of 450 East 52nd Street
in New York City. There is a "G" at the house telephone, but no one answers.

Her daily life in New York is said to be monotonous. She gets up at 7, makes breakfast
herself and is ready to go out when the maid arrives at 9. Every morning she is said to
walk around town until 12.30. She keeps to the quieter streets around First and Second
Avenue. The lunch at home at 1 is followed by a new trip in town. The art galleries on
Madison Avenue are among those places where she has been seen. By the time she gets
home, her maid has left for the day. She rarely goes out after 7. She is said to watch TV
and go to bed around 9.30.

"When Garbo came out without her dark glasses, smiling towards the doorman, our photographer was able to take this shot. Greta Garbo immediately hid her face, but it was too late."

Garbo on her way out of a fashion shop in Paris, October, 1959.

The casual visitor

Garbo's friendship has often been used to make revealing statements about her. This is also the surest way of breaking all ties with her. Today the wall of silence nearest to her is just as high in New York as in her remotely situated residence in Klosters, Switzerland or among her sophisticated circles on the Riviera as among her relatively many Swedish friends.

One of those whom she meets now and then is Kerstin Bernadotte, well-known in Sweden as a journalist and through her marriage with Carl-Johan Bernadotte, a son of Sweden's ruling monarch. They now live in Paris where this photo of Garbo and Mrs Bernadotte was snapped.

A few years ago Kerstin Bernadotte called a dancing school, according to a well-known Stockholm dancing teacher, to arrange lessons for a friend. No one else was allowed to be present at the lessons, which were also to be kept secret. The pupil was Garbo. She is said to have danced enthusiastically.

Get-away

Garbo, in Sweden for the first time in thirteen years, makes a quick get-away from the press at the Stockholm airport in Kerstin Bernadotte's car (1961).

Another long-time friend is artist Einar Nerman who is seen here taking a walk with Garbo in Stockholm.

Garbo above the surface

In her very first film Garbo portrayed a girl in a bathing suit. Not until nearly two decades later did Garbo appear once again in a bathing suit before the camera and this took place in her last film. Another two decades and a telephoto lenses caught Garbo bathing on the Riviera.

On the screen

Once upon a time there was a man by the name of Edgar H. Donne. Born in England, he settled as a farmer in Michigan, where he lived the life of a hermit even though he had some wealth. He owned about 175 acres of land. Edgar H. Donne loved Greta Garbo. He wrote to her but never got an answer. Neighbors have related that he travelled to Hollywood in the hope of catching sight of her. He never saw her.

Edgar H. Donne drew up his will in 1936 as follows: "My land, my securities, my money and other possessions shall go to Greta Louisa Gustafsson, film star, better known by the name of Greta Garbo, and to no one else. If Greta Garbo should become my wife all my possessions are to go to Greta Louisa Donne. Ten years later Edgar H. Donne died at the age of 70. The fortune he left was estimated as $ 15,000 in the form of jewels, securities and cash.

Judge Irving J. Tucker of Allegan, Michigan, tried to get in touch with Garbo to turn over the inheritance. In the meantime he received piles of letters from persons in 12 states and two European countries who had opinions concerning the inheritance or made claims of being Greta Garbo.

Five months later Garbo sent word by letter that she was willing to accept the inheritance and turn it over to a charity. "I never knew Mr Donne", said Garbo. She had a vague memory of having received letters from him. Such letters were normally handled by her secretary. The charity later sold the land to a private enterprise. There was oil in the ground.

The story of Garbo in print and pictures is a remarkable mixture of unawareness of all conceivable human interests. Garbo has remained silent.

"I have never written any sort of article for publication. I have never told my life story to a journalist", she has said. The statement was sufficient to give rise to a number of articles.

"I'll soon become a little old lady if I go on like this", Garbo wrote while still in her twenties. "I live a life that a 70-years-old would appreciate. But I have got the title of 'the mystery'." Today Garbo is an image even for people who have never seen her on the screen.

Garbo has appeared in a total of 27 feature movies. All her work in studios was confined to two decades. The directors, the performers and other such facts about her films have been documented in over fifty books that have been published about her.

Peter the Tramp 1922

The Story of Gösta Berling 1924

The Flesh and the Devil 1926

The Temptress 1926

The Mysterious Lady 1928

A Woman of Affairs 1929

The Torrent 1926

The Street of Sorrow 1925

Love 1927

The Divine Woman 1928

Wild Orchids 1929

The Single Standard 1929

The Kiss 1929

Anna Christie 1930

Romance 1930

Mata Hari 1932

Grand Hotel 1932

As You Desire Me 1932

Conquest 1937

Camille 1936

Inspiration 1931   *Anna Christie 1931*   *Susan Lenox: Her Fall and Rise 1931*

Queen Christina 1933   *The Painted Veil 1934*   *Anna Karenina 1935*

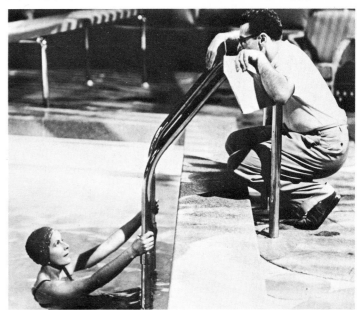

Ninotchka 1939   *The Twofaced Woman 1942*